D1709815

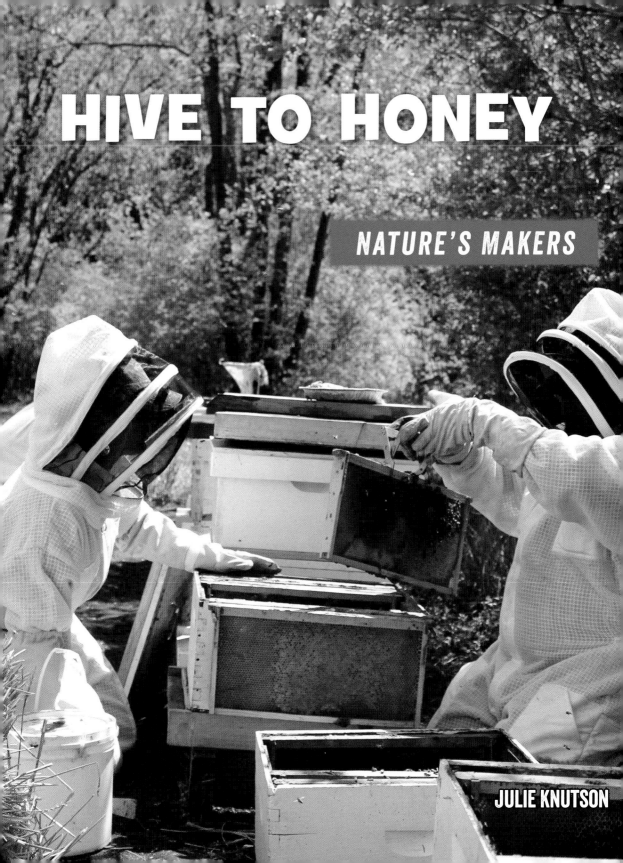

HIVE TO HONEY

NATURE'S MAKERS

JULIE KNUTSON

Published in the United States of America by Cherry Lake Publishing
Ann Arbor, Michigan
www.cherrylakepublishing.com

Content Advisors: Nathan Clarke, owner, Mad Urban Bees; Tim Benedict and Sarah Wells, owners/operators, Orion Organics

Photo Credits: © Courtney Oertel, cover, 1, 11, 18, 20, 22; © Julie Knutson, 5, 26; © SviatlouSS/Shutterstock.com, 6; © Nathan Clarke, 8, 12, 17; © Erin McClendon/Shutterstock.com, 14; © Courtesy of Mad Urban Bees, 25; © rudolfgeiger/Shutterstock.com, 28

Library of Congress Cataloging-in-Publication Data
Names: Knutson, Julie, author. | Knutson, Julie. Nature's makers.
Title: Hive to honey / by Julie Knutson.
Description: Ann Arbor : Cherry Lake Publishing, 2019. | Series: Nature's makers | Includes bibliographical references and index.
Identifiers: LCCN 2018036614| ISBN 9781534143012 (hardcover) | ISBN 9781534140776 (pdf) | ISBN 9781534139572 (pbk.) | ISBN 9781534141971 (hosted ebook)
Subjects: LCSH: Bee culture—Juvenile literature. | Honey—Juvenile literature. | Farms, Small—Juvenile literature.
Classification: LCC SF523.5 .K58 2019 | DDC 638/.1—dc23
LC record available at https://lccn.loc.gov/2018036614

Cherry Lake Publishing would like to acknowledge the work of The Partnership for 21st Century Learning. Please visit www.p21.org for more information.

Printed in the United States of America
Corporate Graphics

ABOUT THE AUTHOR

Julie Knutson is a former teacher who writes from her home in northern Illinois. Researching these books involved sampling a range of farm products, from local honey to heirloom grains to...farm-fresh ice cream! She's thankful to all those who accompanied her on these culinary excursions—most notably to the young ones: Theo, Will, Alex, Ruby, and Olivia.

TABLE OF CONTENTS

CHAPTER 1

Getting from Hive to Honey

Welcome to Madison, state capital of Wisconsin!

This college town swarms with energy. It hosts one of the largest farmers' markets in the United States. It boasts five lakes, over 260 parks, and the largest concentration of Native American **effigy mounds** in the country.

It's also home to Mad Urban Bees, one of the first urban **apiaries** in the country. Travel with us to the Badger State to meet the beekeeper behind the hives, Nathan Clarke. Nathan will teach us about what it takes to own and operate a **commercial** beekeeping business in the middle of a busy city.

Madison is Wisconsin's state capital and second largest city.

Bees pollinate a wide variety of flowers, including fruit-bearing plants.

What's the buzz on honeybees?

These **pollinators** are key to our food supply. Bees fly from plant to plant for **nectar**. In the process, they spread pollen and fertilize the flowering parts of plants. This allows the plant to produce seeds, fruits, or vegetables.

Many of the foods we eat—from almonds to apples—need bees for pollination. Without the work of bees and other pollinators, the stalls at farmers' markets and the shelves at grocery stores would look very different and very colorless.

So what's the buzz on beekeepers?

Nathan is part of a tradition that dates back thousands of years. Beekeepers manage hives to collect beeswax, bee pollen, and honey.

In different times and places, these bee by-products served different purposes. Ancient people sealed and waterproofed pottery with beeswax. The wax was also used to make tools, cosmetics, and medicine. Today, many people take bee pollen to help manage seasonal allergies. And of course, honey has been used for **millennia** as a sweetener.

Nathan's business involves managing everything from hive maintenance to retail operations.

Beekeepers like Nathan see their relationship with bees as beneficial for them, the bees, and the broader **ecosystem**.

Honey of the Pharaohs

Did you know that honey never goes bad?

In 2015, archaeologists unearthed a 3,000-year-old honey pot in an ancient Egyptian tomb. Amazingly enough, the honey in the pot was still edible! This is the world's oldest known sample of the sweet stuff. It shows that honey was enjoyed by the ancients just as it is today.

If you could, would you taste this honey of the pharaohs?

CHAPTER 2

The Road to Beekeeping

How exactly do you become a beekeeper?

For Nathan, the path wasn't direct. As a child, he enjoyed nature. He participated in Scouts and went camping. But did he see himself growing up to be a beekeeper or having an "outdoorsy" career? No. He actually wanted to be an astronaut. And when he grew up, he became a graphic designer.

When Nathan bought his first house, he wanted to be closer to his food source. He became interested in **homesteading**. Today this means growing food for the

This homesteading Illinois family raises chickens, grows vegetables, and cans their own food.

Mad Urban Bees' hives are located in backyards across the Madison area.

family's kitchen in the backyard garden. It also meant keeping animals—of all sizes. Nathan got a nudge from his uncle, who told him, "If you have a yard, you should have bees."

As so began his life as a beekeeper.

After Nathan's daughters were born, he hung up his job as a graphic designer to be a stay-at-home dad. He also got serious about making honey—so much so that he considered turning it into a business. But to do that, you needed more than a single backyard hive.

Research, Write, Discuss!

Does your town allow residents to keep backyard chickens or bees? What are the pros and cons of doing so?

Consider Nathan's perspective. Research other points of view on the topic. Survey people in your neighborhood to gather their thoughts. If you can, talk to community leaders and local farmers for their ideas.

Then, look at the information you have gathered to make up your own mind! Write a short essay expressing your opinion. Share it with a classmate.

What are the pros and cons of keeping backyard chickens?

Not all towns allow residents to host bees on their property. If allowed, the city government has a law that outlines the rules for managing hives. People who want to raise bees need to apply for a license and agree to those rules.

In Madison, the city voted to officially permit backyard beehives in 2012.

In the months leading up to this vote, Nathan began a **crowdfunding** campaign to raise money for his business idea. This business would place hives in the backyards of willing Madison residents. Nathan would care for these hives like a landscaper tends lawns, and collect the honey and wax to turn into products.

"What I do would not be possible without the larger community. My hives are hosted by the community, the bees are foraging in the community, and the people who buy the honey are part of the community."

– Nathan Clarke

CHAPTER 3

What It Takes

As the owner of Mad Urban Bees, Nathan manages from 80 to 100 hives. This land and the bees and plants that live on it are his most crucial **natural resources**. Nathan's knowledge of beekeeping is the needed **human capital** for maintaining the operation.

What **physical capital** is needed to run Mad Urban Bees? Hives! Beekeepers stack wooden boxes one atop another. Then, they place wooden frames inside of them. These frames are where the bees do their work—building honeycombs in which they deposit nectar that turns into honey.

Beekeepers place honey-filled frames from their hives in extractors. The rapid spinning motion of this machine flings the honey out. Then, the honey drips to the base and can be bottled.

Beekeeping suits and veils allow apiarists to remove frames from the hive, check colony health, and extract honey.

Nathan uses other physical capital to get the honey and beeswax. He has a smoker to calm the bees, a beekeeping suit, and an extractor to spin the honey off the comb.

Bees are most active in spring, summer, and fall, when their flowering food sources are richest. This means that Nathan is also most active in the warmer seasons.

During these months, Nathan regularly checks the bees' honey-making progress. Every two to three weeks, he removes the frames from the hives to extract for honey. Before doing this, he takes certain precautions. While honeybees are not aggressive like wasps, they will sting if threatened. Nathan puts on a beekeeping veil and suit to protect his skin. To calm the bees, he sometimes uses a smoker. In nature, smoke signals to the bees that a forest fire might be coming. In response to that threat, the bees stop their busy buzzing and focus on eating. Their genes are programmed to do this to store energy and food, in case they have to flee the hive.

Beekeepers Tim Benedict and Sarah Wells of Illinois' Orion Organics open their hives for the first time in the season to assess how their bees wintered.

These gentle puffs of smoke still the bees and help contain their activity. Nathan can now safely remove the frame. He cuts the layer of wax that the bees use to seal each cell. This wax is used for products like lip **balm**. Then, he extracts the honey with a spinner. The honey trickles through a **sieve**, which filters out any large particles. What's left is a smooth, tasty treat, perfect for topping toast or dipping chicken.

Tending all these hives isn't without challenges. Hive loss—whether from colony collapse or other factors like weather—is a reality that all beekeepers face.

In urban areas like Madison, beekeepers can experience loss due to **parasites**. When this happens, harmful organisms like mites infect and destroy a colony. Weather can slow honey production and cause hive populations to decline. Rain prevents bees from getting out to collect pollen and can drastically reduce a colony's production. And although Nathan and other beekeepers in wintry places wrap and **insulate** their hives, cold temperatures can cause bees to freeze while hibernating.

Rural areas have seen more significant declines in bee populations than cities. Poor nutrition due to the overfarming of certain crops negatively impacts bee health, making them prone to mites and other parasites. Many people also believe that the use of antibiotics—which beekeepers sometimes use to treat bacterial infections in the colony—and certain **pesticides** might harm bees. Combined, these factors might lead to colony collapse.

A healthy hive will have thousands of bees.

As a beekeeper, Nathan tries to minimize the impact of these challenges on the hives. While factors like weather are out of his control, he can strive to provide his bees with a healthy environment through responsible pest management and access to varied pollen sources.

A World of Resources

Nathan is an agricultural **entrepreneur**, which means he coordinates the resources (or **inputs**) to make products (or **outputs**).

Natural Resources—Land and Animals: Natural resources are just what they sound like: materials that come directly from nature. These resources exist without human intervention. Some natural resources, like sun and wind, are **renewable**. Others, like oil and coal, are **nonrenewable**. What natural resources does Mad Urban Bees need to succeed?

Human Resources—Labor: Human resources are the "people" aspect of any operation. In Nathan's case, it's the knowledge, skills, experience, and abilities that he needs to work as a beekeeper and business owner. It also includes any help that he needs from other employees.

Physical Resources—Capital: Physical resources are the things you need to help operate a business, like machines, computers, and buildings. What physical resources does Nathan rely upon?

CHAPTER 4

Meeting Customer Needs

As Mad Urban Bees grew, Nathan drew on his knowledge and experience in graphic design. He used these skills to build a brand. This is one of the key forms of human capital that he brings to his business.

While the logo on the label has changed over the years, it has always visually communicated the *what* and the *where* of his products. The current logo features a gear, which represents the urban environment, with a bee inside of it. To Nathan, it shows the potential for growth and beauty within a city ecosystem.

BEESWAX HAND SALVE

57g

2oz

mad urban bees

Contains: Handmade in Madison, WI, with beeswax from local hives. olive oil, almond oil, and sunflower oil, beeswax, vitamin E.

Nathan drew on his graphic design experience to create Mad Urban Bees' label.

Homegrown DIY Demonstrations

10:30-11:00AM	**Joanne Tooley, Set Up Your Own Worm Bin**
11:30AM-12:00PM	**Nathan Clarke, Introduction to Beekeeping**
12:30-1:00PM	**Lisa Andrewski, Rain Chains**
1:30-2:00PM	**Dave Potter, Quick Mozzarella**
2:30-3:00PM	**Mary Jo Borchardt, DIY Flower Crown**
3:30-4:00 PM	**Faith Andacker, Fermentation Basics**

Nathan and other Madison-area makers frequently teach classes on topics ranging from cheesemaking and flower arranging to beekeeping.

When Mad Urban Bees began, Nathan sold his honey and balms at farmers' markets. This was a **direct-to-consumer** approach. Today, the brand is more established and can be found on the shelves of **retail** stores in Madison. Nathan can also be found teaching people about beekeeping at events like the Madison Mini-Maker Faire.

With Mad Urban Bees, Nathan meets consumer **demand** by supplying products that people want. In the process, he also helps create a healthier environment for pollinators. We can all follow his lead and help our winged friends by providing gardens with a variety of flowering plants.

Bees like to visit a wide variety of flowers.

What's Special About Urban Honey?

Have you ever heard that you should "eat the rainbow"? Good nutrition depends on varying your fruits and vegetables. Choosing produce by color can be one way to eat healthier.

Like humans, bees need variety in their diets. This keeps them healthy and gives their honey unique flavors.

Bees in urban areas like Madison have access to a wider range of flowering trees and plants than their country cousins. This has led some to claim that urban honey has a more complex taste, one that changes with the seasons. The taste depends on what nectar and pollen the bees are eating. These changes are also visible in the color and texture of the honey. It can shift from a pale, thin yellow to a deep, thick orange within a single summer.

Taking Informed Action

What can you do to support honeybee health?

"Stop spraying for dandelions!" says Nathan. Dandelions provide a critical food source for bees early in the season. If you destroy dandelions, you destroy this important food source. In addition, Nathan notes, the effects of weed killers and other lawn chemicals on bees are not fully known.

If the grown-ups in your life aren't on board with natural lawn care, try creating a pollinator-friendly garden. Consider these tips from beekeeper Sarah Wells to attract pollinating insects:

1) **Select the site and the plants:** Bees love nectar- and pollen-rich plants like wildflowers! First, find a good, sunny location for your garden. Then, research plant options through reliable websites like the U.S. Fish & Wildlife Service. Make this a year-round project by starting your seeds indoors in egg cartons in late winter. Nurture the seeds and watch them grow. In the spring, transplant them outside.

2) **Keep bee and butterfly baths in the garden:** "Water is really important, especially in urban areas," Sarah explains. "Bees and butterflies like fresh water in smaller containers. Having water containers out in the flowerbed in the heat of the summer really helps support native pollinators."

3) **Make the garden merry and bright:** Bees are drawn to bright colors, so consider adding brightly painted posts and signs to your garden. But stay away from red! It's the one color that bees cannot see.

GLOSSARY

apiaries (AY-pee-air-eez) places where one or more hives or colonies of bees are kept

balm (BALM) thick lotion that heals and soothes skin

commercial (kuh-MUR-shuhl) related to a business that seeks to make a profit

crowdfunding (KROUD-fuhnd-ing) raising small amounts of money from many people for a project or business

demand (DIH-mand) the want or need for a good or service

direct-to-consumer (duh-REKT TOO kuhn-SOO-mur) selling a product directly to a buyer, as opposed to a store, which may resell it

ecosystem (EE-koh-sis-tuhm) a community of organisms (plants and animals, for example) that interact and interconnect

effigy mounds (EF-ih-jee MOUNDZ) raised piles of dirt built by Native Americans, often representing animals, symbols, or human figures; these mounds sometimes contain human burials

entrepreneur (ahn-truh-pruh-NUR) a person who coordinates resources (natural resources, human capital, physical capital) to create a product and make a profit

homesteading (HOME-sted-ing) small-scale agriculture, sometimes in an urban or suburban environment, which may involve raising livestock or growing food

human capital (HYOO-muhn KAP-ih-tuhl) a person's knowledge and experience that can be used in operating a business

inputs (IN-puts) factors needed to make a product, such as natural resources, human capital, and physical capital

insulate (IN-suh-late) to wrap up to protect from extreme temperatures

millennia (muh-LEN-ee-uh) a period of 1,000 years

natural resources (NACH-ur-uhl REE-sors-iz) materials like land and water that occur in nature that can be used for economic gain

nectar (NEK-tur) sugary fluid produced by plants that is collected by bees and turned into honey

nonrenewable (nahn-rih-NOO-uh-buhl) natural resources that can run out, such as oil or coal

outputs (OUT-puts) the amount of goods produced using various inputs in a given period of time

parasites (PAR-uh-sites) organisms that feed off of another organism

pesticides (PES-tih-sidez) chemicals designed to kill insects

physical capital (FIZ-ih-kuhl KAP-ih-tuhl) resources like machines and equipment that people need to run a business

pollinators (PAH-luh-nate-urz) animals that fertilize plants by moving pollen from the male to female parts of plants

renewable (rih-NOO-uh-buhl) natural resources that never run out, like the sun and wind

retail (REE-tayl) having to do with the sale of goods directly to customers

sieve (SIV) a mesh tool used to separate solids from liquids

FURTHER READING

Burns, Loree Griffin. *The Hive Detectives: Chronicle of a Honey Bee Catastrophe.* New York: Scholastic, 2014.

Wassall, Erika. *Bees Matter.* Minneapolis: ABDO, 2016.

Wilcox, Merrie-Ellen. *What's the Buzz? Keeping Bees in Flight.* Victoria, BC: Orca Book Publishers, 2015.

Woolf, Alex. *You Wouldn't Want to Live Without Bees!* London: Franklin Watts, 2017.

INDEX